RAPID

revision

GCSE
Chemistry for
Double Science

Eileen Ramsden

Hodder & Stoughton

A MEMBER OF THE HODDER HEADLINE GROUP

Using Mind Maps® in your revision

Mind Maps® can be a valuable aid to revision. They help you organise your thoughts in a logical and easy-to-remember format. A sample Mind Map® is provided on page 96. Look at it. Try to use the model to help you revise other topics.

The "Teach Yourself" name and logo are registered trade marks of Hodder & Stoughton Ltd in the UK.

A catalogue record for this title is available from the British Library.

ISBN 0 340 74703 X

First published 1999
Impression number   10 9 8 7 6 5 4 3 2
Year   2000 1999

Editorial, design and production by Hart McLeod, Cambridge

Printed in Great Britain by Circle Services Ltd, Southend, Essex for Hodder & Stoughton Educational, a division of Hodder Headline Plc, 338 Euston Road, London NW1 3BH

Rapid Revision GCSE Chemistry for Double Science

Rapid Revision Planner

4

5

The kinetic theory of matter

The theory states:

Matter is made up of small particles in constant motion.

Solid

In a solid the particles are close together and attract one another strongly. They vibrate about fixed positions in a regular three-dimensional structure. When the solid is heated, the particles gain energy and move energetically. They may break away from the structure and move freely: the solid has melted.

Liquid

In a liquid the particles are slightly further apart than in a solid. They are free to move about, although forces of attraction exist between them. When a liquid is heated some particles gain enough energy to break away from the other particles and become a gas.

Gas

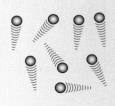

Most of a gas is space, through which the particles move at high speed. There are only very small forces of attraction between the particles.

Change of state

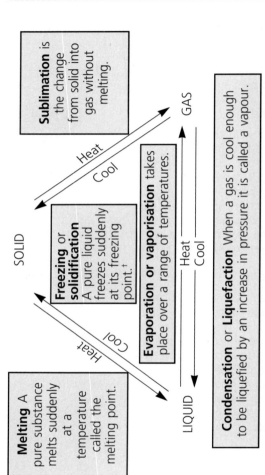

Sublimation is the change from solid into gas without melting.

GAS

Heat

Cool

SOLID

Freezing or **solidification** A pure liquid freezes suddenly at its freezing point. †

Evaporation or vaporisation takes place over a range of temperatures.

Heat

Cool

Heat

Cool

Melting A pure substance melts suddenly at a temperature called the melting point.

LIQUID

Condensation or **Liquefaction** When a gas is cool enough to be liquefied by an increase in pressure it is called a vapour.

† The melting point of a solid and the freezing point of a liquid are the same temperature.

What does the kinetic theory explain?

Dissolving of a solid Particles separate from the solid and spread out through the solvent – dissolve – to form a solution.

Diffusion of a gas Particles of gas are far apart and can move freely. As particles move through the container occupied by the gas, the gas diffuses – spreads evenly through all the space available.

Gas density Gases have much lower densities than solids and liquids because the particles in a gas are so widely separated.

Brownian motion Smoke particles suspended in the air move to and fro as they are bombarded from all directions by gas molecules.

Changes of state

Melting The particles of a solid gain enough energy to move independently as a liquid.

Evaporation or vaporisation Attractive forces exist betweeen the molecules in a liquid. Some molecules with energy above average break away from the attraction of other molecules and escape into the vapour phase. The average energy of the molecules that remain is lower than before: the liquid has cooled.

See also   • **Rapid Revision Physics, Topic 2,** p. 21

Matter and the kinetic theory

Matter

Questions

1 How can you tell whether a solid is pure from its melting point?

2 What is the difference between evaporation and boiling?

3 What happens to the heat that is supplied to a solid to make it melt?

4 Explain why (a) you can smell perfume (b) a spoonful of sugar can sweeten a cup of tea (c) vegetables cook faster in a pressure cooker (d) gases can be easily compressed.

Answers

1 The temperature remains steady while all the pure solid melts. **2** Evaporation = change from liquid to gas; boiling = change from liquid to gas at the boiling point of the liquid. **3** The heat energy is used to separate the particles against the forces of attraction between them. **4** (a) The liquid vaporises and gas molecules diffuse into your nose. (b) Particles of sugar leave the solid and dissolve – spread through the liquid tea. (c) The boiling point of water is >100°C when the pressure > 1 atm. (d) There are vast spaces between the particles in a gas; they can move closer together.

Elements, Compounds, Mixtures

Elements

Elements are pure substances that cannot be split up into simpler substances.

Physical properties of metallic and non-metallic elements

Metallic elements	Non-metallic elements
Solids except for mercury	Solids and gases – except bromine
Dense, hard	Most of the solid elements are softer than metals – except diamond
A smooth metallic surface is shiny	Most are dull – except diamond
The shape can be changed without breaking e.g. by hammering and by stretching	Many are brittle: they break when a force is applied
Conduct heat	Poor thermal conductors
Good electrical conductors	Poor electrical conductors – except graphite
Sonorous	Not sonorous

Elements

Chemical properties of metallic and non-metallic elements

Metallic elements	Non-metallic elements
Many displace hydrogen from dilute acids to form salts.	Do not react with acids except for oxidising acids, e.g. concentrated sulphuric acid.
The metal is the cation (positive ion) in the salts, e.g. Na^+, Ca^{2+}.	Form anions (negative ions) e.g. S^{2-} and oxoanions, e.g. SO_4^{2-}.
Form basic oxides and hydroxides, e.g. Na_2O, $NaOH$, CaO, $Ca(OH)_2$.	Form acidic oxides, e.g. CO_2, SO_2, or neutral oxides, e.g. CO, NO.
The chlorides are ionic solids, e.g. $MgCl_2$, $AlCl_3$.	The chlorides are covalent volatile liquids, e.g. SCl_2, PCl_3.
Few form hydrides.	Form stable hydrides, e.g. HBr, H_2S.

Structures of elements
Individual molecules e.g. oxygen O_2.
Molecular structures e.g. solid iodine with a structure composed of I_2 molecules.
Giant molecules e.g. diamond and graphite, allotropes of the element carbon.

Compounds and Mixtures

Compounds	Mixtures
A compound is a pure substance that contains two or more elements chemically combined. It contains the elements in fixed proportions by mass, e.g. magnesium oxide always contains 60% by mass of magnesium.	A mixture can contain its components in any proportions.
When a compound is made a chemical reaction takes place. Often heat is taken in or given out.	No chemical change takes place when a mixture is made.
The properties of a compound are different from those of the components.	A mixture has the same properties as its components.
A compound can be split into its elements or into simpler compounds only by a chemical reaction, e.g. thermal decomposition – by heat, and electrolysis – by electricity.	A mixture can be separated into parts by various methods; see Topic 3.

Symbols, Formulas, Equations

The **symbol** of an element is a letter or two letters which stand for one atom of the element, e.g. aluminium Al, iron Fe.

The **formula** of a compound is composed of the symbols of the elements present and numbers which give the ratio in which the atoms are present, e.g. sulphuric acid H_2SO_4, silicon(IV) oxide SiO_2, ammonium sulphate $(NH_4)_2SO_4$.

To **write an equation** for a chemical reaction:

1 Write a word equation for the reaction,

e.g. calcium + water→
        hydrogen + calcium hydroxide solution

2 Put in the symbols for the elements and formulas for the compounds.

$Ca + H_2O \rightarrow H_2 + Ca(OH)_2$

3 Put in the state symbols.

$Ca(s) + H_2O(l) \rightarrow H_2(g) + Ca(OH)_2(aq)$

4 Balance the equation. Make the number of atoms of each element on the left-hand side equal the number on the right-hand side. You can multiply a symbol or a formula by two or three or another numeral. You can never alter a formula.

$Ca(s) + 2H_2O(l) \rightarrow H_2(g) + Ca(OH)_2(aq)$

Elements, Compounds, Mixtures

Questions

1 Say whether the elements T–Z are metallic or non-metallic:
(a) T forms ions T^{2+} (b) U forms an acidic oxide, UO_2 (c) V reacts with dilute hydrochloric acid (d) W forms a crystalline chloride WCl_2 (e) X forms a stable hydride HX (f) Y forms a basic oxide Y_2O_3 (g) Z forms ions ZO_4^{3-}.

2 List four physical properties in which metallic elements and non-metallic elements differ.

3 The ore magnetite is mined in many different places. How would you find out whether it is a compound or a mixture?

4 How many atoms are present in $CuSO_4.5H_2O$?

5 Balance the following equation and insert state symbols:
$Na_2CO_3 + HCl \rightarrow NaCl + CO_2 + H_2O$

Answers

1 (a) m (b) n—m (c) m (d) m (e) n—m (f) m (g) n—m. **2** See table on page 11. **3** Find out whether it always has the same composition by mass. **4** 21 **5** $Na_2CO_3(s) + 2HCl(aq) \rightarrow 2NaCl(aq) + CO_2(g) + H_2O(l)$

Methods of Separating Substances

3

All the materials we use come from the Earth's crust and atmosphere. Methods have to be found for separating the substances we want from a mixture of substances.

Separating a soluble solid from an insoluble solid

Filtration

Add a solvent, e.g. water, and stir to dissolve one solid. Filter. The insoluble solid is left on the filter paper as the residue. Evaporate the filtrate to obtain the soluble solid.

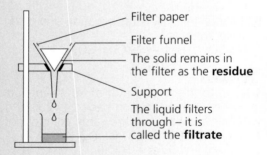

Filter paper

Filter funnel

The solid remains in the filter as the **residue**

Support

The liquid filters through – it is called the **filtrate**

Separating two or more solids by chromatography

Chromatography on an extract from green leaves

The diagram shows chromatography on a solution of the pigments in green leaves. The solvent is ethanol. The pigments separate because they travel through the chromatography paper at different speeds.

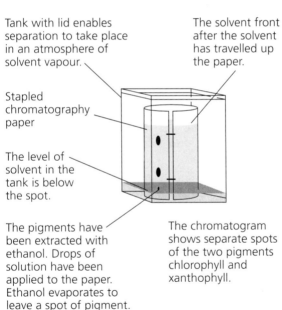

Tank with lid enables separation to take place in an atmosphere of solvent vapour.

Stapled chromatography paper

The level of solvent in the tank is below the spot.

The pigments have been extracted with ethanol. Drops of solution have been applied to the paper. Ethanol evaporates to leave a spot of pigment.

The solvent front after the solvent has travelled up the paper.

The chromatogram shows separate spots of the two pigments chlorophyll and xanthophyll.

Separating a solvent and a solute in a solution

A laboratory distillation apparatus

Heat the solution in the distillation apparatus shown. The solvent distils over and condenses in the receiver. The solute remains in the distillation flask.

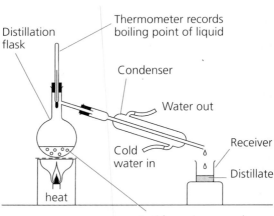

Thermometer records boiling point of liquid

Distillation flask

Condenser

Water out

Cold water in

Receiver

Distillate

heat

Anti-bumping granules assist smooth boiling

Separating two miscible liquids

Apparatus for fractional distillation

In fractional distillation the lower boiling point liquid, e.g. ethanol, b.p. 78°C, distils over first. Then the temperature rises as the liquid with the higher boiling point, e.g. water, b.p. 100°C, distils over. Continuous (non-stop) fractional distillation is used to separate crude petroleum oil into a number of useful fuels – see Topic 14.

The fractionating column has a large surface area. Vaporisation followed by condensation of the vapour takes place many times on the surface of the fractionating column. The liquid with the lowest boiling point reaches the top of the column first and distils over.

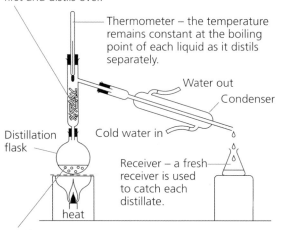

Thermometer – the temperature remains constant at the boiling point of each liquid as it distils separately.

Water out

Condenser

Distillation flask

Cold water in

Receiver – a fresh receiver is used to catch each distillate.

heat

Anti-bumping granules

See also   • p. 86 **Petroleum fractions and their uses**

Separating two immiscible liquids

The mixture of immiscible liquids, e.g. oil and water, is poured into a separating funnel. It settles into two layers. The tap is opened to let the bottom layer run into a receiver and then closed. The top layer is run into a different receiver.

Questions

1 What method would you use to separate the following mixtures
   (a) (i) a mixture of two solids (ii) two solids dissolved in the same solution
   (b) (i) a mixture of a solid and a liquid
       (ii) a solution of a solid in a liquid
   (c) (i) two miscible liquids (ii) two immiscible liquids?
2 How are diesel oil and lubricating oil obtained from crude oil?
3 How can a food chemist test a food colouring to find out whether it contains any forbidden additives?

Answers

1 (a) (i) Use a difference in solubility.
(ii) Chromatography. (b) (i) Filter. (ii) Crystallise to obtain the solid. Distil to obtain the liquid.
(c) (i) Fractional distillation. (ii) A separating funnel. 2 Fractional distillation. 3 Obtain a chromatogram of the colouring and compare with those of forbidden additives.

The Structure of the Atom 4

Protons, neutrons and electrons

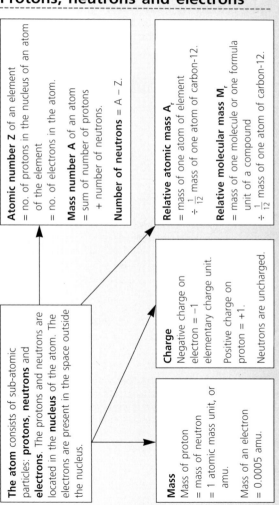

The atom consists of sub-atomic particles: **protons**, **neutrons** and **electrons**. The protons and neutrons are located in the **nucleus** of the atom. The electrons are present in the space outside the nucleus.

Mass
Mass of proton
= mass of neutron
= 1 atomic mass unit, or amu.

Mass of an electron
= 0.0005 amu.

Charge
Negative charge on electron = −1 elementary charge unit.

Positive charge on proton = +1.

Neutrons are uncharged.

Atomic number Z of an element
= no. of protons in the nucleus of an atom of the element
= no. of electrons in the atom.

Mass number A of an atom
= sum of number of protons + number of neutrons.

Number of neutrons = A − Z.

Relative atomic mass A_r
= mass of one atom of element
$\div \frac{1}{12}$ mass of one atom of carbon-12.

Relative molecular mass M_r
= mass of one molecule or one formula unit of a compound
$\div \frac{1}{12}$ mass of one atom of carbon-12.

The arrangement of particles

The arrangement of protons, neutrons and electrons in the atom is shown in the figure. The electrons which are moving in orbits far away from the nucleus have more energy than those close to the nucleus.

An atom

The nucleus occupies a tiny volume in the centre of the atom. It consists of protons and neutrons.

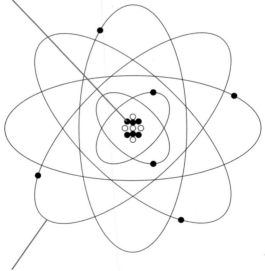

The electrons occupy the space surrounding the nucleus. They repel the electrons of neighbouring atoms. The electrons are in constant motion, moving round the nucleus in circular paths called orbits.

The arrangement of electrons

A group of electron orbits of similar energy is called a **shell.** The first shell can hold 2 electrons, the second shell 8 electrons, the third shell 18 electrons (an inner group of 10 and an outer group of 8). In the outermost shell of any atom, the maximum number of electrons is 8.

If you know the atomic number of an element you can work out the arrangement of electrons. The lower energy orbits are filled first.

The arrangement of electrons in the carbon atom (2.4)

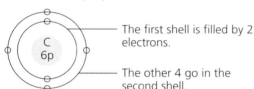

The first shell is filled by 2 electrons.

The other 4 go in the second shell.

The arrangement of electrons in the magnesium atom (2.8.2)

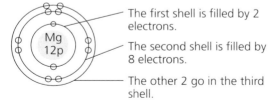

The first shell is filled by 2 electrons.

The second shell is filled by 8 electrons.

The other 2 go in the third shell.

Isotopes

Some elements consist of **isotopes** – forms of the same element which have the same number of protons but different numbers of neutrons: the same atomic number but different mass numbers. The isotopes of carbon are:

Mass number → 12   14

                  C ← Symbol and   C

Atomic number → 6   6

Questions

1 Explain why, although an atom is made of charged particles, the atom is uncharged.

2 Write the symbols, with mass numbers and atomic numbers, for phosphorus (atomic no. 15, mass no. 31) and potassium (atomic no. 19, mass no. 39).

3 State the arrangements of electrons in the atoms of B (atomic no. 5), F (atomic no. 9), Al (atomic no. 13), S (atomic no. 16) and Ca (atomic no. 20).

Answers

1 number of protons = number of electrons.
2 $^{31}_{15}P$ $^{39}_{19}K$. **3** B (2.3), F (2.7), Al (2.8.3), S (2.8.6), Ca (2.8.8.2).

What happens when compounds conduct electricity?

When compounds conduct **electricity** changes happen at the **electrodes**. For example, a solution of copper chloride gives a deposit of copper at the negative electrode and a stream of chlorine at the positive electrode.

- The explanation is that copper chloride consists of copper ions – positively charged particles of copper – and chloride ions – negatively charged particles of chlorine.
- The copper ion carries two units of positive charge, Cu^{2+}, whereas the chloride ion carries one unit of negative charge, Cl^-. Copper chloride contains two chloride ions for every copper ion so that the charges balance and the formula is $CuCl_2$.
- Solid copper chloride does not conduct electricity because the ions are not free to move. The ions are held in a three-dimensional crystal structure. When the salt is dissolved in water the ions become free to move, the solution conducts electricity and electrolysis occurs.
- There is another way of giving the ions freedom to move – to melt the solid. The electrolysis of molten sodium chloride is used for the extraction of sodium.

See also • p. 31 **Ionic bonding**

Electrolysis of copper(II) chloride solution with carbon electrodes

Electrons flow through the external circuit from the positive electrode to the negative electrode

copper(II) chloride solution

Chloride ions are attracted to the positive electrode. The positive charge enables the electrode to take electrons from chloride ions, discharging them to form chlorine atoms. Chlorine atoms then combine to form molecules. The electrode process is:

$Cl^-(aq) \rightarrow Cl(g) + e^-$

followed by $2Cl(g) \rightarrow Cl_2(g)$

Copper ions are attracted to the negative electrode. The negative charge on the electrode is due to the presence of electrons, and copper ions take electrons and are discharged to become copper atoms. The electrode process is:

$Cu^{2+}(aq) + 2e^- \rightarrow Cu(s)$

Sodium chloride solution

The electrolysis of sodium chloride solution is used commercially to obtain the important products **sodium hydroxide**, **hydrogen** and **chlorine**. The water in the solution is ionised to a very small extent to give hydrogen ions and hydroxide ions.

• At the cathode hydrogen ions are discharged in preference to sodium ions.
Cathode process: $H^+(aq) + e^- \rightarrow H(g)$
followed by $2H(g) \rightarrow H_2(g)$
As hydrogen ions are discharged more water molecules ionise to replace them, more hydrogen ions are discharged, and the concentration of hydroxide ions increases.
• At the anode chlorine is evolved – see $CuCl_2$ on page 26.
• The solution of sodium chloride gradually turns into a solution of sodium hydroxide.

Copper(II) sulphate solution

Copper forms at the cathode and **oxygen** at the anode.

• At the anode hydroxide ions are present due to the ionisation of water molecules. They are discharged in preference to sulphate ions.
Anode process: $OH^-(aq) \rightarrow OH(aq) + e^-$
followed by $4OH(aq) \rightarrow O_2(g) + 2H_2O(l)$
• At the cathode copper is deposited – see $CuCl_2$ on page 26.
• Hydrogen ions are also formed by the dissociation of water and the solution gradually turns into a solution of sulphuric acid.

Electrolysis

Which ions are discharged?

Discharge of anions

Sulphate ions and nitrate ions are very difficult to discharge. In solutions of these ions, hydroxide ions are discharged in preference to form oxygen.

Discharge of cations

The ions of very reactive metals, e.g. sodium and potassium, are difficult to discharge. In solutions of these ions, hydrogen ions are discharged instead.

The ions of less reactive metals, e.g. copper and lead, are easier to discharge. In a solution which contains a mixture of metal ions, the ions are discharged in order of the reactivity of the metals, least reactive first, e.g. Cu^{2+} ions are discharged in preference to Zn^{2+} ions.

Electrodes which take part

When copper(II) sulphate is electrolysed with copper electrodes, at the cathode copper is deposited as before. The copper anode, instead of discharging SO_4^{2-} ions or OH^- ions, gains electrons by ionising Cu atoms:
$$Cu(s) \rightarrow Cu^{2+}(aq) + 2e^-$$
Copper is dissolved from the anode and deposited on the cathode.

The products of electrolysis of some electrolytes

Electrolyte	Cathode (negative electrode)	Anode (positive electrode)
Sodium chloride molten	Sodium $Na^+(l) + e^- \rightarrow Na(l)$	Chlorine $Cl^-(l) \rightarrow Cl(g) + e^-$ $2Cl(g) \rightarrow Cl_2(g)$
Sodium chloride solution	Hydrogen $H^+(aq) + e^- \rightarrow H(g)$ $2H(g) \rightarrow H_2(g)$	Chlorine $Cl^-(aq) \rightarrow Cl(g) + e^-$ $2Cl(g) \rightarrow Cl_2(g)$
Copper(II) sulphate solution	Copper $Cu^{2+}(aq) + 2e^- \rightarrow Cu(s)$	Oxygen $OH^-(aq) \rightarrow OH(aq) + e^-$ $4OH(aq) \rightarrow O_2(g) + 2H_2O(l)$
Copper (II) sulphate solution, with copper electrodes	Copper is discharged $Cu^{2+}(aq) + 2e^- \rightarrow Cu(s)$	Copper dissolves $Cu(s) \rightarrow Cu^{2+}(aq) + 2e^-$
Dilute sulphuric acid	Hydrogen $H^+(aq) + e^- \rightarrow H(g)$ $2H(g) \rightarrow H_2(g)$	Oxygen $OH^-(aq) \rightarrow OH(aq) + e^-$ $4OH(aq) \rightarrow O_2(g) + 2H_2O(l)$

Applications of electrolysis

Extraction of metals from their ores

Sodium, potassium, calcium and **magnesium** are obtained by electrolysis of molten anhydrous chlorides.

Aluminium

From the ore bauxite, $Al_2O_3.2H_2O$, anhydrous aluminium oxide is obtained. It is dissolved in molten cryolite, Na_3AlF_3 at 1000°C before electrolysis in a steel cell. The carbon lining of the cell is the cathode, at which aluminium collects. At the carbon anodes oxygen is evolved.

Purification of Copper

In the purification of copper, the electrolysis of copper(II) sulphate with copper electrodes is used. Copper dissolves from the anode (a slab of impure copper), and pure copper is deposited on the cathode.

Electroplating

The object to be plated is made the cathode in a solution of a salt of the metal. The anode is made of the plating metal.
1. A cheaper metal may be coated with a more beautiful and more expensive metal.
2. To prevent steel from rusting it is electroplated with nickel and chromium.
3. Food cans are made of iron plated with tin, which is not corroded by food juices.
4. A layer of zinc is applied to iron in the manufacture of galvanised iron.

See also • p. 72 **Methods used for the extraction of metals from their ores.**

When atoms combine, the electrons in the outer shell take part in the formation of bonds. The stability of the noble gases to chemical change is believed to be due to the stability of the full outer shell of 8 electrons (2 for helium). When atoms react they gain, lose or share electrons to attain an outer shell of 8 electrons.

Ionic bonding

Sodium burns in chlorine to form sodium chloride

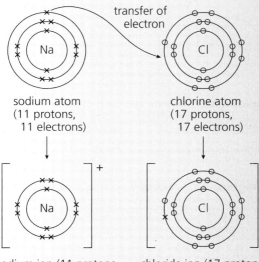

transfer of electron

sodium atom
(11 protons,
11 electrons)

chlorine atom
(17 protons,
17 electrons)

sodium ion (11 protons, 10 electrons, one unit of positive charge) with same arrangement of electrons as the noble gas neon

$Na \rightarrow Na^+ + e^-$

chloride ion (17 protons, 18 electrons, one unit of negative charge) with same arrangement of electrons as the noble gas argon

$Cl + e^- \rightarrow Cl^-$

Ionic bonding continued

An electrostatic force of attraction exists between oppositely charged ions. This force is called an **ionic bond** or **electrovalent bond**. The ions Na⁺ Cl⁻ are part of a **giant ionic structure** (a crystal). The ions cannot move out of their positions in the structure, and the crystal cannot conduct electricity. When the solid is melted or dissolved, the ions become free to move and conduct electricity (see Topic 5).

Magnesium + fluorine → magnesium fluoride

One magnesium atom gives away two electrons to become the ion.

$$Mg \rightarrow Mg^{2+} + 2e^-$$

Each of the two fluorine atoms gains one electron to become a fluoride ion.

$$F + e^- \rightarrow F^-$$

Magnesium + oxygen → magnesium oxide

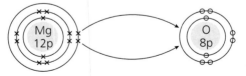

A magnesium atom gives away two electrons to form a Mg^{2+} ion.

$$Mg \rightarrow Mg^{2+} + 2e^-$$

An oxygen atom gains two electrons to become an oxide ion O^{2-}.

$$O + 2e^- \rightarrow O^{2-}$$

Covalent bonding

When non-metallic elements combine, both want to gain electrons; neither wants to form positive ions. They combine by sharing electrons. A shared pair of electrons is a **covalent bond**. The shared pair of electrons is attracted to both nuclei and bonds the two nuclei together. If two pairs of electrons are shared the bond is a **double bond**.

Example 1 Hydrogen fluoride HF

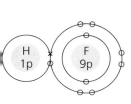

The hydrogen atom shares its electron with the fluorine atom. H has a full shell of 2 electrons, the same arrangement as helium.

The fluorine atom shares one of its electrons with the hydrogen atom. F has a full shell of 8 electrons, the same arrangement as neon.

Example 2 Water H_2O

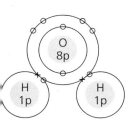

Two hydrogen atoms each share an electron with an oxygen atom. Each hydrogen atom has an outer shell of 2 electrons, and the oxygen atom has an outer shell of 8 electrons.

Ionic compounds

The **strong electrostatic attraction** between ions of opposite charge is an **ionic bond**. An ionic compound is composed of a **giant regular structure of ions**. This regular structure makes ionic compounds **crystalline**. The strong forces of attraction between ions make it difficult to separate the ions, and ionic compounds therefore have **high melting and boiling points**.

Ionic compounds are **electrolytes** – they conduct electricity when molten or in solution and are **electrolysed** (split up) in the process. Covalent compounds are **non-electrolytes**.

Ionic bonding

Ionic compounds are formed when a metallic element combines with a non-metallic element. An **ionic bond** is formed by **transfer of electrons** from one atom to another to form ions.

Atoms of **metallic elements** form positive ions (cations). Elements in Groups 1, 2 and 3 of the Periodic Table form ions with charges +1, +2 and +3, e.g. Na^+, Mg^{2+}, Al^{3+}. Atoms of **non-metallic elements** form negative ions (anions). Elements in Groups 6 and 7 of the periodic table form ions with charges -2 and -1, e.g. O^{2-} and Cl^-.

Covalent compounds

Covalent bonding

Atoms of non-metallic elements combine with other non-metallic elements by **sharing pairs of electrons** in their outer shells. A shared pair of electrons is a **covalent bond**.

The **maximum number** of covalent bonds that an atom can form is equal to the **number of electrons in the outer shell**. An atom may not use all its outer electrons in bond formation.

There are **three types of covalent substances.**

• Many covalent substances are composed of small individual molecules with only very small forces of attraction between molecules, e.g. the gases HCl, SO_2, CO_2, CH_4.

• Some covalent substances consist of small molecules with weak forces of attraction between molecules, e.g. the volatile liquid ethanol, C_2H_5OH, and solid carbon dioxide.

• Some covalent substances consist of giant molecules, e.g. quartz (silicon(IV) oxide). These substances have high melting and boiling points.

35

The Chemical Bond

Questions

1 The elements E and Cl have the electron arrangements E (2.8.2) and Cl (2.8.7). Explain what happens to atoms of E and Cl when they combine, and give the formula of the compound.

2 The element X has the electron arrangement (2.7). Sketch the arrangement of electrons in an atom of X and in the molecule X_2.

3 (a) What are the particles in a crystal of sodium chloride? (b) What holds the particles together?

4 Draw the arrangement of electrons in a molecule of hydrogen chloride.

5 Give examples of covalent substances which are (a) individual molecules (b) molecular solids (c) giant molecules.

Answers

1 Atoms of E each lose two electrons → E^{2+}. Atoms of Cl gain one electron each → Cl^-; ECl_2. **2** X has 2 electrons in inner shell, 7 in outer shell. In X_2 the two atoms share one pair of electrons (page 32). **3** (a) Positive ion. **4** Similar to HF (page 33) but Cl has electron arrangement 2.8.7 whereas F has 2.7. **5** (a) e.g. CH_4 and $CO_2(g)$. (b) e.g. $I_2(s)$ and $CO_2(s)$. (c) e.g. Diamond and SiO_2.

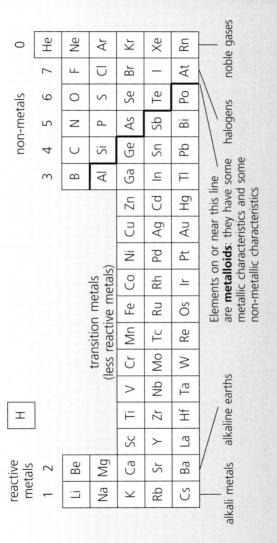

The Periodic Table

		reactive metals		transition metals (less reactive metals)													non-metals						noble gases
	1	2												3	4	5	6	7	0
																			He
	Li	Be												B	C	N	O	F	Ne
	Na	Mg												Al	Si	P	S	Cl	Ar
	K	Ca	Sc	Ti	V	Cr	Mn	Fe	Co	Ni	Cu	Zn	Ga	Ge	As	Se	Br	Kr
	Rb	Sr	Y	Zr	Nb	Mo	Tc	Ru	Rh	Pd	Ag	Cd	In	Sn	Sb	Te	I	Xe
	Cs	Ba	La	Hf	Ta	W	Re	Os	Ir	Pt	Au	Hg	Tl	Pb	Bi	Po	At	Rn

H

alkali metals

alkaline earths

Elements on or near this line are **metalloids**: they have some metallic characteristics and some non-metallic characteristics

halogens

The alkali metals and the alkaline earths

Some reactions of Groups 1 and 2

Metal	Reaction with air	Reaction with water	Reaction with dilute hydrochloric acid	Trend
Group 1 the alkali metals				
Lithium	Burn vigorously to form the strongly basic oxide M_2O which dissolves in water to give the strong alkali MOH.	React vigorously to form hydrogen and a solution of the strong alkali MOH.	The reaction is dangerously violent.	Reactivity increases →
Sodium				
Potassium				
Rubidium				
Caesium				
Group 2 the alkaline earths				
Beryllium	Burn to form the strongly basic oxides MO, which are sparingly soluble or insoluble.	Reacts very slowly. Burns in steam.	React readily to give hydrogen and a salt, e.g. MCl_2.	Reactivity increases →
Magnesium		{ React readily to form hydrogen and the alkali $M(OH)_2$.		
Calcium				
Strontium				
Barium				

Halogens

Some reactions of the halogens

Halogen	State at room temperature	Reaction with sodium	Reaction with iron	Trend
Fluorine	Gas	Explosive	Explosive	
Chlorine	Gas	Heated sodium burns in chlorine to form sodium chloride.	Reacts vigorously with hot iron to form iron(III) chloride.	
Bromine	Liquid	Reacts less vigorously to form sodium bromide.	Reacts less vigorously to form iron(III) bromide.	
Iodine	Solid	Reacts less vigorously than bromine to form sodium iodide.	Reacts less vigorously than bromine to form iron(II) iodide.	Reactivity increases ↑

Transition metals	Reaction with air	Reaction with water	Reaction with dilute hydrochloric acid	Trend
Iron	When heated, form oxides without burning. The oxides and hydroxides are weaker bases than those of Groups 1 and 2 and are insoluble.	Iron rusts slowly. Iron and zinc react with steam to form hydrogen and the oxide. Copper does not react.	Iron and zinc react to give hydrogen and a salt. Copper does not react.	Less reactive than Groups 1 and 2. Compounds are coloured; they are used as catalysts.
Zinc				
Copper				

The Periodic Table – Questions

1 In what order are elements listed in the Periodic Table?

2 (a) What are the 'noble gases'? (b) What do they have in common?

3 In which group of the Periodic Table would you place each of the following?
X a metallic element which reacts slowly with water to give a strongly alkaline solution,
Y a non-metallic element which reacts vigorously with sodium to give a salt NaY.
Z a metallic element which reacts rapidly with water to give a flammable gas and an alkaline solution.

Answers 1 Increasing atomic number. **2**(a) The very unreactive gases in Group 0. (b) They have full outer shells of electrons. Very few chemical reactions. **3** X 2, Y 7, Z 1.

Acids

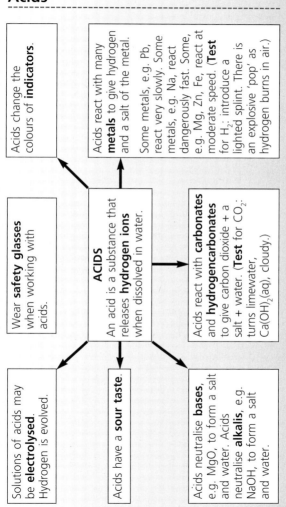

Acids change the colours of **indicators**.

Acids react with many **metals** to give hydrogen and a salt of the metal.

Some metals, e.g. Pb, react very slowly. Some metals, e.g. Na, react dangerously fast. Some, e.g. Mg, Zn, Fe, react at moderate speed. (**Test** for H_2: introduce a lighted splint. There is an explosive 'pop' as hydrogen burns in air.)

Wear **safety glasses** when working with acids.

ACIDS
An acid is a substance that releases **hydrogen ions** when dissolved in water.

Acids react with **carbonates** and **hydrogencarbonates** to give carbon dioxide + a salt + water. (**Test** for CO_2: turns limewater, $Ca(OH)_2(aq)$, cloudy.)

Solutions of acids may be **electrolysed**. Hydrogen is evolved.

Acids have a **sour taste.**

Acids neutralise **bases**, e.g. MgO, to form a salt and water. Acids neutralise **alkalis**, e.g. NaOH, to form a salt and water.

Bases

Wear **safety glasses** when working with bases.

Bases change the colour of **indicators**.

Bases react with solutions of many **metal salts** to precipitate $M(OH)_2(s)$ or $M(OH)_3(s)$. (Most metal hydroxides are insoluble.)

BASES
e.g. sodium hydroxide, NaOH, a strong base.
e.g. ammonia, NH_3, a weak base.

Definitions
A **base** is a substance that reacts with an acid to form a salt and water only, e.g. magnesium oxide + hydrochloric acid →
magnesium chloride + water.
An **alkali** is a soluble base, e.g. sodium hydroxide.

Bases have a 'soapy feel'. They are used as **degreasing agents**. When boiled with sodium hydroxide, fats are converted into **soaps** (an industrial process).

Bases **neutralise all acids**, e.g. HCl, H_2SO_4 and others, to form water and a salt. e.g. NaCl, Na_2SO_4, NH_4Cl, $(NH_4)_2SO_4$.

Neutralisation and indicators

Neutralisation is the combination of hydrogen ions (from an acid) and hydroxide ions (from an alkali) or oxide ions (from an insoluble base) to form water. In the process a salt is formed.

e.g. hydrochloric acid + sodium hydroxide $\rightarrow$ sodium chloride + water

$$HCl(aq) + NaOH(aq) \rightarrow NaCl(aq) + H_2O(l)$$

    acid   +   alkali $\rightarrow$ salt   + water

e.g. sulphuric acid + copper(II) oxide $\rightarrow$ copper(II) sulphate + water

$$H_2SO_4(aq) + CuO(s) \rightarrow CuSO_4(aq) + H_2O(l)$$

    acid   +   base $\rightarrow$ salt   + water

Indicators

Indicator	Acidic colour	Neutral colour	Alkaline colour
Litmus	Red	Purple	Blue
Phenolphthalein	Colourless	Colourless	Red
Methyl orange	Red	Yellow	Yellow

Universal indicator turns many different colours in solutions of different pH

Some useful salts

Sodium chloride NaCl. Rock salt is spread on roads in winter. Pure salt is used to flavour and to preserve foods. Electrolysis of brine gives chlorine, hydrogen and sodium hydroxide.

Sodium carbonate-10-water $Na_2CO_3.10H_2O$, 'washing soda', a water softener.

Sodium hydrogencarbonate $NaHCO_3$, 'baking soda', a rising agent.

Calcium sulphate-$\frac{1}{2}$-water $CaSO_4.\frac{1}{2}H_2O$, plaster of Paris.

Silver bromide AgBr is used in black and white photographic film.

Iron(II) sulphate-7-water $FeSO_4.7H_2O$ is used as a remedy for anaemia.

Barium sulphate $BaSO_4$ is used in 'barium meals'.

Copper(II) sulphate $CuSO_4$ is used as a fungicide on grapes and potatoes.

Calcium fluoride CaF_2 is added to toothpastes to protect against tooth decay.

NPK fertilisers contain ammonium nitrate NH_4NO_3, ammonium sulphate $(NH_4)_2SO_4$, calcium phosphate $Ca_3(PO_4)_2$ and potassium chloride KCl.

Methods of making salts

Soluble salts

Method 1 acid + metal $\rightarrow$ salt + hydrogen

Warm the acid in a beaker. Add an excess of the metal. When no more hydrogen is evolved the reaction is complete.

Method 2 acid + metal oxide $\rightarrow$ salt + water

Warm the acid in a beaker. Add an excess of the metal oxide. When the solution no longer turns blue litmus red the reaction is complete.

Method 3 acid + metal carbonate $\rightarrow$
$\qquad$ salt + water + carbon dioxide

Take some acid in a beaker. Add an excess of the metal carbonate. When no more carbon dioxide is evolved, the reaction is complete.

Then for all three methods filter and evaporate the filtrate until crystals form.

Method 4 acid + alkali $\rightarrow$ salt + water

Titrate to find the exact volumes of alkali and acid needed for neutralisation.

Insoluble salts: precipitation

Insoluble salts are made by mixing two solutions, e.g.
barium chloride + sodium sulphate $\rightarrow$ barium sulphate(s) + sodium chloride
The precipitate is separated by filtering or centrifuging.

Acids, Bases and Salts

Questions

1 Define (a) an acid (b) a base (c) an alkali.
2 The following pairs of substances react to form salts. Name each salt and say what else is formed (a) potassium hydroxide + sulphuric acid (b) ammonia + nitric acid (c) zinc + hydrochloric acid (d) copper(II) oxide + sulphuric acid (e) calcium nitrate + sodium carbonate (f) magnesium + sulphuric acid (g) calcium carbonate + hydrochloric acid.
3 Lead(II) iodide is insoluble. Lead(II) nitrate and all sodium salts are soluble. Suggest two solutions that could be mixed to make lead(II) iodide, and write a word equation for the reaction.

Answers

1 (a) See page 41, (b) see page 42 (c) see page 42. 2 (a) potassium sulphate + water (b) ammonium nitrate (c) zinc chloride + hydrogen (d) copper(II) sulphate + water (e) calcium carbonate + sodium nitrate (f) magnesium sulphate + hydrogen (g) calcium chloride + carbon dioxide + water. 3 lead(II) nitrate(aq) + sodium iodide(aq) $\rightarrow$ lead(II) iodide(s) + sodium nitrate(aq).

Oxygen

Oxygen makes up 21% of air. All plants and animals need oxygen for respiration.

Uses of pure oxygen

- Aeroplanes which fly at high altitude and all space flights carry oxygen.
- Deep-sea divers carry cylinders which contain a mixture of oxygen and helium.
- An oxy-acetylene torch (which burns ethyne, C_2H_2, in oxygen) has a very hot flame (4000°C) and is used for welding and cutting metals.
- Cast iron contains carbon, which is burnt off in a stream of oxygen to make steel.
- Oxygen is pumped into polluted rivers and lakes.

Reactions of oxygen

Many elements react with oxygen to form oxides; see Table on page 48. Combination with oxygen is one type of **oxidation**.
Combustion is oxidation in which energy is given out.
Burning is combustion accompanied by a flame.
Fuels are substances which undergo combustion.

Test for oxygen

A glowing wooden splint lowered into oxygen starts to burn brightly because all substances burn more rapidly in oxygen than in air.

See also   • p. 85 **Fossil Fuels**   **47**

Air

Reactions of oxygen with some elements

Element	Observation	Product	Action of product on water
Calcium (metal)	Burns with a red flame	Calcium oxide (white solid)	Dissolves → strongly alkaline solution
Copper (metal)	Turns black without burning	Copper(II) oxide (black solid)	Insoluble
Iron (metal)	Burns with yellow sparks	Iron oxide Fe_3O_4 (blue-black solid)	Insoluble
Magnesium (metal)	Burns with a white flame	Magnesium oxide (white solid)	Dissolves slightly → alkaline solution
Sodium (metal)	Burns with a yellow flame	Sodium oxide (white solid)	Dissolves readily → strongly alkaline solution
Carbon (non-metal)	Glows red	Carbon dioxide (invisible gas)	Dissolves slightly → weakly acidic solution
Sulphur (non-metal)	Burns with a blue flame	Sulphur dioxide (fuming gas)	Dissolves readily → strongly acidic solution

Oxides

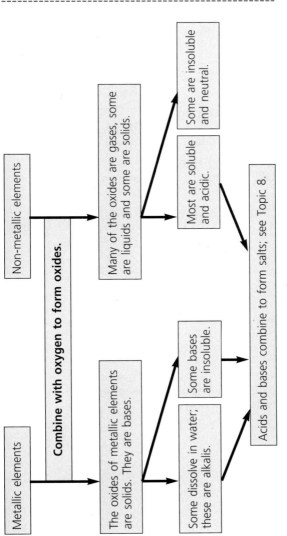

Metallic elements → **Combine with oxygen to form oxides.** ← **Non-metallic elements**

The oxides of metallic elements are solids. They are bases.

Some dissolve in water; these are alkalis.

Some bases are insoluble.

Many of the oxides are gases, some are liquids and some are solids.

Some are insoluble and neutral.

Most are soluble and acidic.

Acids and bases combine to form salts; see Topic 8.

Oxidation and reduction

Oxidation = gain of oxygen or loss of hydrogen.

Reduction = loss of oxygen or gain of hydrogen.

An **oxidising agent** gives oxygen or takes hydrogen.

Definition in terms of electron transfer –

Oxidation **I**s **L**oss of electrons

Reduction **I**s **G**ain of electrons

OIL RIG

A **reducing agent** takes oxygen or gives hydrogen.

Oxidation and reduction occur together, e.g. lead(II) oxide + hydrogen → lead + water

$$PbO(s) + H_2(g) \rightarrow Pb(s) + H_2O(l)$$

Loss of oxygen: reduction

$$PbO(s) + H_2(g) \rightarrow Pb(s) + H_2O(l)$$
oxidising reducing
agent   agent

Gain of oxygen: oxidation

It is better to call these reactions **oxidation–reduction reactions** or **redox reactions**.

Nitrogen

Nitrogen makes up 78% of air. It does not take part in many chemical reactions. Many uses of nitrogen depend on its lack of reactivity.

- Liquid nitrogen is used in the fast-freezing of foods.

- Many foods are packed in an atmosphere of nitrogen to prevent oxidation.

- Oil tankers and grain silos are flushed out with nitrogen as a precaution against fire.

Manufacture of ammonia

Under the conditions of the Haber Process, nitrogen will combine with hydrogen.

nitrogen + hydrogen $\rightleftharpoons$ ammonia
$$N_2(g) + 3H_2(g) \rightleftharpoons 2NH_3(g)$$

The reaction is reversible. The percentage of ammonia in the mixture is increased by a high pressure and a low temperature. The reaction is very slow at a low temperature, and industrial plants operate at 200 atm and 500°C with a catalyst (iron with promoters, e.g. Al_2O_3) to speed up the reaction.

Nitric acid is made by oxidising ammonia made by the Haber Process.
NPK fertilisers Mixtures of ammonium nitrate, ammonium phosphate and potassium chloride are sold as **NPK fertilisers**.

The nitrogen cycle

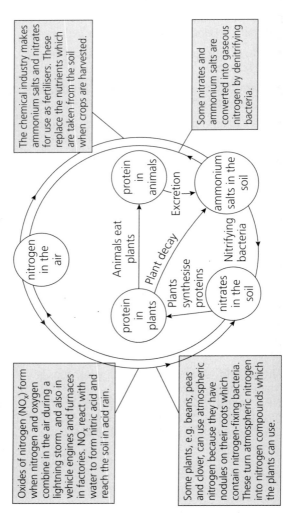

The chemical industry makes ammonium salts and nitrates for use as fertilisers. These replace the nutrients which are taken from the soil when crops are harvested.

Some nitrates and ammonium salts are converted into gaseous nitrogen by denitrifying bacteria.

protein in animals

Excretion

ammonium salts in the soil

nitrogen in the air

Animals eat plants

Plant decay

Nitrifying bacteria

protein in plants

Plants synthesise proteins

nitrates in the soil

Oxides of nitrogen (NO_x) form when nitrogen and oxygen combine in the air during a lightning storm, and also in vehicle engines and furnaces in factories. NO_x react with water to form nitric acid and reach the soil in acid rain.

Some plants, e.g. beans, peas and clover, can use atmospheric nitrogen because they have nodules on their roots which contain nitrogen-fixing bacteria. These turn atmospheric nitrogen into nitrogen compounds which the plants can use.

See also • Rapid Revision Biology, Topic 1, p. 18

Carbon dioxide and the carbon cycle

Plants are able to make sugars by the process of **photosynthesis**.

catalysed by chlorophyll
carbon dioxide + water + sunlight → glucose + oxygen

The energy of sunlight is converted into the energy of the chemical bonds in glucose. Animals obtain energy by **cellular respiration**:

glucose + oxygen → carbon dioxide + water + energy

Uses of carbon dioxide

Soft 'fizzy' drinks are made by dissolving carbon dioxide in water under pressure and adding sugar and flavourings.

Solid carbon dioxide sublimes. It is used as the refrigerant 'dry ice' or Dricold.

Carbon dioxide is used in fire extinguishers because it does not support combustion and is denser than air.

Test for carbon dioxide

Carbon dioxide reacts with a solution of calcium hydroxide (limewater) to form a white precipitate of calcium carbonate.

carbon dioxide + calcium hydroxide → calcium carbonate + water
$$CO_2(g) + Ca(OH)_2(aq) \rightarrow CaCO_3(s) + H_2O(l)$$

See also   • **Rapid Revision Biology, Topic 3,** p. 39, 59

The carbon cycle

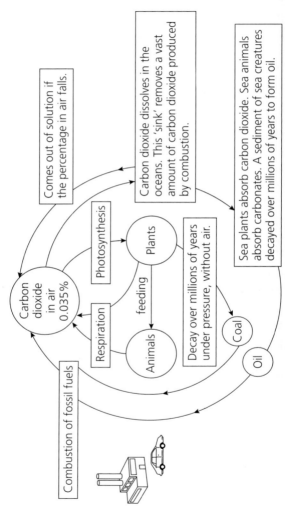

Comes out of solution if the percentage in air falls.

Carbon dioxide dissolves in the oceans. This 'sink' removes a vast amount of carbon dioxide produced by combustion.

Sea plants absorb carbon dioxide. Sea animals absorb carbonates. A sediment of sea creatures decayed over millions of years to form oil.

Photosynthesis

Plants

Carbon dioxide in air 0.035%

feeding

Respiration

Animals

Decay over millions of years under pressure, without air.

Coal

Oil

Combustion of fossil fuels

See also • Rapid Revision Biology, Topic 1, p. 19

The greenhouse effect

The Earth receives radiation from the Sun and also radiates heat into space. Carbon dioxide and water vapour reduce the escape of heat energy from the Earth by means of the **greenhouse effect**. Without these 'blankets' of water vapour and carbon dioxide, the temperature of the Earth's surface would be −20°C, and life on Earth would be impossible.

The combustion of fossil fuels is causing an increase in the level of atmospheric carbon dioxide at a rate which could raise the average temperature of the Earth. One result would be that the massive ice caps of the Arctic and Antarctic regions would slowly begin to melt. The levels of oceans would rise and coastal areas would be flooded. A rise in temperature could decrease food production over vast areas. Other 'greenhouse gases' are methane, chlorofluorocarbons (CFCs), nitrogen oxides and ozone.

The noble gases

Helium, neon, argon, krypton and xenon are the noble gases; see page 37.

- Helium is used in airships because of its low density.
- Neon and other noble gases are used in illuminated signs.
- Argon is used to fill light bulbs.

See also • **Rapid Revision Biology, Topic 1,** p. 24

55

The problem of pollution

Carbon monoxide

Source Vehicle engines where it is formed by the incomplete combustion of petrol.

Effects Odourless and poisonous. Low levels cause headaches and dizziness.

Solutions to the problem Fitting vehicles with catalytic converters, using fuels which burn more cleanly than hydrocarbons, e.g. ethanol.

Sulphur dioxide

Sources Extraction of metals from ores, burning of coal and oil in power stations.

Effects Contributes to bronchitis and lung diseases. It is a cause of acid rain.

Acid rain causes costly damage to building materials, e.g. limestone, concrete, cement and metal and to the natural environment.

Solutions to the problem Power stations can reduce sulphur dioxide emission

- by washing coal with a solvent to remove sulphur
- by purifying fuel oil
- by flue gas desulphurisation, FGD, of the exhaust gases of power stations
- by pulverised fluidised bed combustion, PFBC, in furnaces which remove sulphur dioxide as formed.

See also • **Rapid Revision Biology, Topic 1**, p. 23

Smoke, Dust and Grit

Sources Natural sources, power stations, incinerators, industries and vehicles.

Solutions Removing particles by filtering or using sprays of water or using electrostatic precipitators which attract particles to charged plates.

Hydrocarbons

Source Decay of plant material (85%); from vehicles (15%); in sunlight, hydrocarbons react with oxygen and oxides of nitrogen to form **photochemical smog**.

Solution Use a catalyst to promote complete combustion in vehicle engines.

Oxides of nitrogen

Source Power stations, factories and vehicles emit nitrogen monoxide NO, and nitrogen dioxide, NO_2. Nitrogen dioxide contributes to the formation of acid rain.

Solution The presence of a catalyst (platinum) brings about the reaction:

nitrogen monoxide + carbon monoxide $\rightarrow$ nitrogen + carbon dioxide

$$2NO(g) + 2CO(g) \rightarrow N_2(g) + 2CO_2(g)$$

Catalytic converters which are now fitted in the exhausts of cars reduce the emission of oxides of nitrogen in this way. Unleaded petrol must be used because lead compounds in the exhaust gases stop the catalyst working.

Questions

1 (a) Give two industrial uses for oxygen.
(b) Describe a test for oxygen.
2 Name elements which burn in the following ways:
a blue flame → an acidic gas
b yellow flame → invisible gas
c bright white flame → basic solid
d red glow → invisible gas
3 Name two processes which turn atmospheric nitrogen into compounds.
4 (a) Name two processes which take carbon dioxide out of the atmosphere.
(b) How would you test an invisible gas to find out if it is carbon dioxide?
5 Name four atmospheric pollutants and state one source of each.

Answers

1 (a) E.g. oxy-acetylene flame, steel-making, sewage treatment, combatting pollution. (b) It makes a glowing splint burn more brightly.
2 a = sulphur b = sodium c = magnesium d = carbon. **3** E.g. lightning, vehicle engines, Haber process, fixation by bacteria. **4** (a) E.g. dissolving in oceans, photosynthesis. (b) Pass through limewater: $Ca(OH)_2(aq)$. A white precipitate shows that the gas is carbon dioxide. **5** E.g. carbon monoxide – motor vehicles, sulphur dioxide and hydrocarbons – combustion of coal and oil, NO_x – motor vehicles, dust – mining, factories, fires.

The water cycle

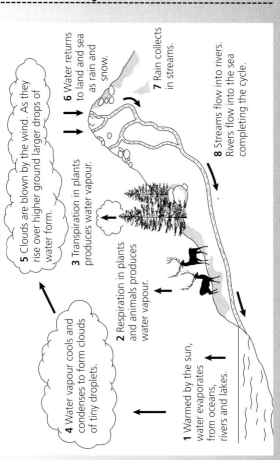

1 Warmed by the sun, water evaporates from oceans, rivers and lakes.

2 Respiration in plants and animals produces water vapour.

3 Transpiration in plants produces water vapour.

4 Water vapour cools and condenses to form clouds of tiny droplets.

5 Clouds are blown by the wind. As they rise over higher ground larger drops of water form.

6 Water returns to land and sea as rain and snow.

7 Rain collects in streams.

8 Streams flow into rivers. Rivers flow into the sea completing the cycle.

Water underground

Rain water dissolves **carbon dioxide** as it falls through the air and natural rain water is therefore weakly acidic. In limestone regions, acidic rain reacts with rocks containing calcium carbonate and magnesium carbonate.

calcium carbonate + water + carbon dioxide
→ calcium hydrogencarbonate

$CaCO_3(s) + H_2O(l) + CO_2(aq) \rightarrow Ca(HCO_3)_2(aq)$

Over a period of thousands of years, enough of these carbonates has been dissolved out of the rocks to form underground caverns.

The reverse reaction can take place. In an underground cavern, dissolved calcium hydrogencarbonate can turn into tiny crystals of calcium carbonate. Over thousands of years, these tiny crystals can build up into stalactites and stalagmites.

Dissolved oxygen

The **solubility** of oxygen in water is ten parts per million. Water-living animals and plants depend on this dissolved oxygen. Aerobic bacteria which feed on plant and animal debris in the water also use dissolved oxygen. If the oxygen is used up, for example by oxidising untreated sewage, the aerobic bacteria die. Anaerobic bacteria take over to produce unpleasant-smelling decay products.

Tests for water

Water turns white anhydrous copper(II) sulphate blue.

copper(II) sulphate + water → copper(II) sulphate-5-water

$$CuSO_4(s) + 5H_2O(l) \rightarrow CuSO_4.5H_2O(s)$$

Water turns blue anhydrous cobalt(II) chloride pink.

cobalt(II) chloride + water → cobalt(II) chloride-2-water

$$CoCl_2(s) + 2H_2O(l) \rightarrow CoCl_2.2H_2O(s)$$

Water of crystallisation gives these hydrates their colour and crystalline form.

Tests for pure water

Pure water boils at 100°C at 1 atm and freezes at 0°C at 1 atm.

Methods of obtaining pure water

Distillation (see Topic 3)

Deionisation – water passes through an ion exchange column. This contains a resin which takes cations (M^+) and anions (A^-) out of the water and replaces them with H^+ and OH^- ions. Then H^+ and OH^- ions combine to form water.

Pollution of water
Pollution by industry

Many industrial firms have their factories on the banks of rivers and estuaries and discharge waste into the water. The Environment Agency watches over the quality of rivers and prosecutes polluters. It does not have authority over coastal waters and estuaries, which receive much sewage and industrial waste.

Pollution by sewage

Much sewage is discharged into rivers and estuaries without being treated. Dozens of British beaches fail to meet European Community standards because they have too high a level of coliform bacteria and faecal bacteria in the water.

Pollution by agriculture

Sometimes a farmer applies more fertiliser than a crop can use. Rain washes the excess fertiliser out of the soil, and it accumulates in ground water. The water industry uses ground water as a source of drinking water. There is concern that nitrates in drinking water can damage health.

Excess fertiliser may be carried into a lake. This accidental enrichment of the water is called **eutrophication**. Weeds flourish and algae form a thick mat of **algal bloom**. When algae die and decay they use up dissolved oxygen and fish die.
Pesticides may enter lakes and become part of a food chain.

See also   • Rapid Revision Biology, Topic 1, p. 24

Pollution of water continued

Thermal pollution

Industries take water from rivers to use as a coolant and return it at a higher temperature. The solubility of oxygen is lower at the higher temperature. At the same time the **biochemical oxygen demand** increases as fish and aerobic bacteria become more active.

Pollution by lead

For centuries, water pipes were made of lead. Eventually it was realised that lead dissolves slowly in water and that lead and its compounds are poisonous. Some parts of the UK still have lead water pipes. Little lead dissolves now because a layer of insoluble lead carbonate has formed inside the pipes.

Pollution by oil

Modern oil tankers are huge. If a tanker has an accident at sea, oil is spilt, and a huge oil slick floats on the surface of the ocean. It is very slowly oxidised by air and decomposed by bacteria. While the oil slick remains, it poisons fish and glues the feathers of seabirds together so they cannot fly. When the oil slick washes ashore it fouls beaches.

Methods of dealing with oil slicks are: disperse with powerful detergents, sink it by spreading with e.g. powdered chalk, absorb it in e.g. straw and polystyrene, place booms in the water to prevent oil from spreading.

Water

Questions

1 Name three processes which send water vapour into the atmosphere.

2 Explain (a) why rainwater is weakly acidic (b) how weakly acidic rainwater leads to the formation of underground caves in limestone regions.

3 (a) State (i) a test to find out whether a liquid contains water (ii) a test to show whether a liquid is pure water. (b) Give two methods of purifying water.

4 What is 'thermal pollution' of water? Why is it harmful?

5 (a) Why do some lakes develop an algal bloom? (b) Why is algal bloom less common in rivers? (c) What harm does algal bloom do to a lake?

Answers

1 Transpiration, respiration, vaporisation.
2 (a) Dissolved CO_2 (b) Acids attack $CaCO_3$ (limestone). **3** (a) (i) Anhydrous copper(II) sulphate turns blue; or anhydrous cobalt(II) chloride turns pink; (ii) b.p. 100°c, m.p. 0°C. (b) Distillation and deionisation. **4** Raising the temperature reduces solubility of oxygen.
5 (a) Fertiliser washes into the lakes and nourishes plant growth. (b) Fertiliser is diluted by fresh water in a river; it builds up in a lake. (c) Dead algae decay and use up dissolved oxygen depriving fish of oxygen.

The structure of the Earth

hydrosphere (water covers 70% of Earth's surface)

atmosphere – gaseous layer

outer core – liquid rock, density 10–12 g/cm^3, composed of nickel and iron, Earth's magnetic field arises here

crust (5–40 km) – solid rock, density 2.0–3.0 g/cm^3

lithosphere (50–100 km) – outer mantle and crust

mantle – a thick layer of solid rock, density 3.4–5.5 g/cm^3. Parts of the mantle move slowly

Mohorovičić discontinuity (Moho) – the boundary between the crust and the mantle

inner core – solid rock at very high temperature and pressure, density 12–18 g/cm^3, composed of nickel and iron

Plate tectonics

Earthquakes and volcanoes occur in belts of activity, which run along chains of high mountains and along oceanic ridges (chains of high mountains beneath the sea). Why do earthquakes and volcanoes occur in some parts of Earth's crust and not others? The theory of **plate tectonics** holds that the lithosphere is made up of a number of separate **plates**. Movements in the mantle carry the plates along at a rate of about 5 cm a year. When plates push against each other stress builds up. The plates may bend more and more until suddenly and violently they spring back into shape. Then the shock is felt as an earthquake. The energy which the mantle uses in moving comes from the decay of radioactive elements.

Destructive boundary Plates collide and **subduction** occurs. The edge of the oceanic plate slides beneath the continental plate, and the ocean shrinks.

Constructive boundary Lava erupts from volcanoes along the oceanic ridges and cools to form a new oceanic crust. It causes **sea-floor spreading**, making the ocean wider.

Conservative boundary Two plates slide past one another, no lithosphere is added or lost.

The movement of plates

Material is subducted from plates at oceanic trenches and added at oceanic ridges. As the mantle moves, the plates which it carries move as though on a **conveyer belt**. The continents on the plates have been moving for thousands of millions of years and have already travelled thousands of kilometres.

Movement of plates on the 'conveyor belt'

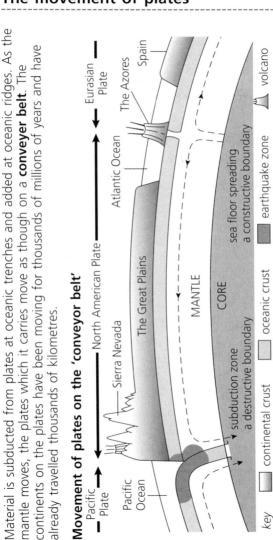

key:
continental crust
oceanic crust
earthquake zone
volcano

---→ very slow movements of mantle under plates

Types of rock

Igneous rocks

Volcanic lava crystallises above Earth's surface to form **extrusive igneous rocks** and below Earth's surface to form **intrusive igneous rocks**. The faster the rate of cooling, the smaller are the crystals, e.g. basalt, granite and pumice.

Sedimentary rocks

Rocks are worn down by weathering and by erosion. Fragments are carried by winds, ice and rivers and deposited as a **sediment** on a sea shore or ocean floor or desert. As material builds up, pressure on the sediment turns it into a sedimentary rock. Sedimentary rocks may contain fossils. If a rock contains the fossils of creatures which were alive 250 million years ago, the rock must be 250 million years old, e.g. limestone, coal sandstone.

Metamorphic rocks

Metamorphic rocks are formed from igneous and sedimentary rocks at high temperature or high pressure, e.g. marble and slate.

Rock cycle

The rock cycle is the interconversion between igneous, sedimentary and metamorphic rocks.

The rock cycle

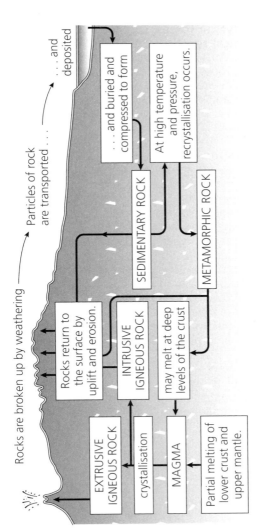

The landscape

Rocks are broken down by **weathering** due to **physical forces**, e.g. wind and rain, and **chemical reactions**, e.g. when limestone reacts with acidic rainwater. **Erosion** happens when rocks are broken down and the particles are carried away, e.g. by water or wind, and when minerals in the rocks dissolve in water. Weathering and erosion shape the landscape.

Questions
1 Name the following zones of the Earth: (a) made of nickel and iron (b) lies beneath ocean floors (c) forms continents (d) gaseous (e) where Earth's magnetism arises (f) the outermost solid zone.
2 Name the types of rock formed (a) when lava solidifies (b) by compressing deposits of solid particles (c) by the action of heat and pressure on types (a) and (b).
3 (a) How could a geologist find the age of a sedimentary rock? (b) Under what conditions do sedimentary rocks turn into metamorphic rocks?

Answers
1 Refer to page 65. 2 Refer to page 68. 3 (a) Date the fossils in it. (b) High pressure and temperature.

The chemical reactions of metals

Metal	Reaction when heated in oxygen	Reaction with cold water	Reaction with dilute hydrochloric acid
Potassium Sodium Lithium Calcium Magnesium	Burn to form the oxides	Displace hydrogen; form alkaline hydroxides	React dangerously fast to form hydrogen and the metal chloride
Aluminium*		Reacts slowly	Displace hydrogen; form metal chlorides
Zinc Iron		Do not react, except for slow rusting of iron – all react with steam	
Tin Lead	Slowly form oxides without burning	Do not react even with steam	React very slowly to form hydrogen and the metal chloride
Copper Silver Gold Platinum	Do not react		Do not react

*Aluminium forms a surface layer of aluminium oxide and only shows its true reactivity if this layer is removed.

The reactivity series

The table shows part of the reactivity series of metals. The method chosen for extracting a metal from its ore depends on the position of the metal in the reactivity series.

Part of the reactivity series of metals

Metal	Symbol	Trends
Potassium	K	
Sodium	Na	
Lithium	Li	Increase in reactivity
Calcium	Ca	
Magnesium	Mg	
Aluminium	Al	Increase in the ease with which metals react to form ions
Zinc	Zn	
Iron	Fe	
Tin	Sn	
Lead	Pb	
Copper	Cu	
Silver	Ag	
Gold	Au	
Platinum	Pt	

Methods used for the extraction of metals from their ores

Metal	Extraction methods
Potassium Sodium Calcium Magnesium	Anhydrous chloride is melted and electrolysed.
Aluminium	Molten anhydrous oxide is electrolysed.
Zinc Iron Lead	Sulphides are roasted to give oxides which are reduced with carbon; oxides are reduced with carbon.
Copper	Sulphide ore is heated with a controlled volume of air.
Silver Gold	Found 'native' (as the free metals).

Predictions from the reactivity series

We can predict the reaction between two elements from their positions in the series.

Competition between metals for oxygen

When aluminium is heated with iron(III) oxide, aluminium displaces iron because aluminium is above iron in the reactivity series.

aluminium + iron(III) oxide → iron + aluminium oxide

This very exothermic reaction (the **thermit reaction**) yields molten iron, and is used to weld pieces of metal together.

Discharge of ions in electrolysis

When metal ions are discharged in electrolysis, the ions of metals high in the reactivity series are difficult to discharge and the ions of metals low in the reactivity series are easy to discharge. For example,

- when a solution containing copper ions and iron ions is electrolysed, copper is formed at the cathode, while iron ions remain in solution

- when a solution containing copper ions and silver ions is electrolysed, silver is discharged at the cathode, while copper ions remain in solution.

See also • p. 28 Which ions are discharged?

Predictions from the reactivity series continued

Competition between metals to form ions

A metal which is higher in the reactivity series will displace a metal which is lower in the reactivity series from a salt.

copper + silver nitrate solution $\rightarrow$
silver + copper(II) nitrate solution

Compounds and the reactivity series

The higher a metal is in the reactivity series the more ready it is to form compounds and the more difficult it is to split up its compounds.

Oxides

• The oxides of metals which are low in the reactivity series, e.g. copper and lead, are reduced by hydrogen and by carbon.

• Iron oxides are reduced by carbon monoxide.

• The oxides of metals which are high in the reactivity series, e.g. aluminium, are not reduced by hydrogen or carbon or carbon monoxide.

• The oxides of silver and mercury, which are very low in the reactivity series, decompose when heated.

• The sulphates, carbonates and hydroxides of metals of lower reactivity than sodium decompose on heating.

Extraction of iron in a blast furnace

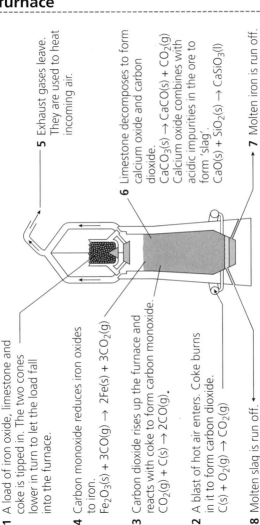

1 A load of iron oxide, limestone and coke is tipped in. The two cones lower in turn to let the load fall into the furnace.

2 A blast of hot air enters. Coke burns in it to form carbon dioxide.
$C(s) + O_2(g) \rightarrow CO_2(g)$

3 Carbon dioxide rises up the furnace and reacts with coke to form carbon monoxide.
$CO_2(g) + C(s) \rightarrow 2CO(g)$.

4 Carbon monoxide reduces iron oxides to iron.
$Fe_2O_3(s) + 3CO(g) \rightarrow 2Fe(s) + 3CO_2(g)$

5 Exhaust gases leave. They are used to heat incoming air.

6 Limestone decomposes to form calcium oxide and carbon dioxide.
$CaCO_3(s) \rightarrow CaCO(s) + CO_2(g)$
Calcium oxide combines with acidic impurities in the ore to form 'slag'.
$CaO(s) + SiO_2(s) \rightarrow CaSiO_3(l)$

7 Molten iron is run off.

8 Molten slag is run off.

Iron and steel

The iron that comes out of the blast furnace is called **cast iron**. It contains 3–4% of carbon which lowers the melting point, making cast iron easier to melt and mould than pure iron. Objects with complicated shapes can be made by casting, e.g. the engine blocks of motor vehicles. The carbon content makes cast iron brittle. **Steel** is made from iron by burning off carbon and other impurities in a stream of oxygen. A number of elements may be added to give different types of steel – chromium and nickel in stainless steels, tungsten in steel for high-speed cutting tools, vanadium in steel for springs.

Rusting of iron and steel

Iron and steel corrode to form rust, $Fe_2O_3.nH_2O$, when attacked by water, air and acid. The carbon dioxide in the air provides acidity. If the water contains salts, rusting takes place faster. In a warm climate, rusting is more rapid.

Some of the methods used to prevent or delay rusting are:

- a coat of paint, a film of oil, a coat of metal, e.g. chromium, zinc, tin

- alloying with chromium or nickel to form stainless steels

- sacrificial protection, allowing a more reactive metal to corrode instead of iron.

Metals and alloys

Questions

1 What method is used to extract the following from their ores (i) iron (ii) aluminium?

2 Copy and complete these word equations, if there is no reaction, write 'n.r.'.
   (a) magnesium + sulphuric acid →
   (b) copper + oxygen →
   (c) silver + hydrochloric acid →
   (d) tin + water →
   (e) aluminium + iron(III) oxide →
   (f) iron + aluminium oxide →
   (g) carbon monoxide + iron(III) oxide →
   (h) carbon monoxide + aluminium oxide →
   (i) zinc + copper(II) sulphate solution →

3 A metal X, displaces another metal Y, from a solution of a salt of Y. X is displaced by a metal Z, from a solution of a salt of X. List the metals in order of reactivity with the most reactive first.

4 The following metals are listed in order of reactivity, with the most reactive first.
   Na Mg Al Zn Fe Pb Cu Hg Au
   List the metals which
   (a) occur as free elements in Earth's crust
   (b) react at an observable speed with cold water
   (c) react with steam but not with cold water
   (d) react at an observable speed with dilute acids
   (e) react dangerously fast with dilute acids
   (f) displace lead from lead(II) nitrate solution.

5 Give examples of objects which are protected from rusting by (a) paint (b) oil (c) chromium plating.

6 (a) What happens when (i) the tin on a tin-plated steel can is scratched (ii) the zinc on a zinc-plated steel can is scratched? (b) Why are food cans tin-plated?

7 Give an example of sacrificial protection.

8 List three advantages of recycling metal objects.

Answers

1 (i) Reduce the oxide with carbon monoxide. (ii) Electrolyse the molten anhydrous oxide.

2 (a) hydrogen + magnesium sulphate (b) copper(II) oxide (c) n.r. (d) n.r. (e) iron + aluminium oxide (f) n.r. (g) iron + carbon dioxide (h) n.r. (i) copper + zinc sulphate.

3 Z > X > Y **4** (a) Cu Hg Au (b) Na Mg (c) Zn Fe (d) Mg Zn Fe (e) Na (f) Mg Al Zn Fe.

5 (a) bridges, ships (b) machinery (c) taps, trim on cars. **6** (a) (i) The iron starts to rust. (ii) The iron does not rust. (b) Tin is non-toxic; zinc is toxic. **7** e.g. Zinc bars on the hull of a ship corrode and protect the ship from rusting. Magnesium attached to underground pipes corrodes and leaves the pipes intact.

8 The Earth's resources of metals are limited. Less energy is needed for recycling than for extracting metals from their ores. Mining damages the landscape.

Particle size

The marble chips and acid reaction

In the reaction between marble chips and acid,

calcium + hydrochloric → carbon + calcium + water
carbonate   acid   dioxide   chloride

$$CaCO_3(s) + 2HCl(aq) \rightarrow CO_2(g) + CaCl_2(aq) + H_2O(l)$$

As carbon dioxide is given off the mass of the reacting mixture gradually decreases. The rate of the reaction can be found by plotting a graph of mass against time.

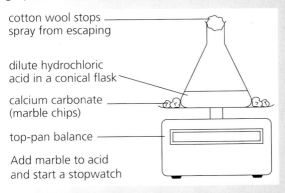

cotton wool stops spray from escaping

dilute hydrochloric acid in a conical flask

calcium carbonate (marble chips)

top-pan balance

Add marble to acid and start a stopwatch

It is found that the smaller the marble chips, the faster is the reaction. In general, the reaction between a solid and a liquid is speeded up by using smaller particles of the solid. The reason is that it is the atoms or ions at the surface of the solid that react first, and the ratio of surface area/mass is greater for small particles than for large particles.

Concentration

The acid and thiosulphate reaction

A precipitate of sulphur is formed in the reaction:

sodium thiosulphate + hydrochloric acid →
    sulphur + sulphur dioxide +
    sodium chloride + water

$$Na_2S_2O_3(aq) + 2HCl(aq) \rightarrow$$
$$S(s) + SO_2(g) + 2NaCl(aq) + H_2O(l)$$

Reaction rate measurement

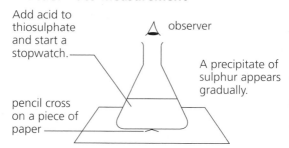

Add acid to thiosulphate and start a stopwatch.

observer

A precipitate of sulphur appears gradually.

pencil cross on a piece of paper

Note the time when the precipitate is thick enough to block your view of a cross on a piece of paper. Repeat for various concentrations of acid and for various concentrations of thiosulphate. The results show that for this reaction

- Rate is proportional to concentration of thiosulphate
- Rate is proportional to concentration of acid.

Explanation In a concentrated solution, the reacting particles (ions or molecules) collide more frequently.

Pressure, Temperature and Light

Pressure

An increase in pressure increases the rates of
reactions between gases. As the molecules
are pushed more closely together, they react
more rapidly.

Temperature

The reaction between thiosulphate and acid
(see page 80) can be used to study the effect
of temperature on the rate of a reaction. This
reaction goes twice as fast at 30°C as it does
at 20°C. At higher temperatures ions have
more kinetic energy and collide more often
and more vigorously, giving them a greater
chance of reacting.

Light

Heat is not the only form of energy that
speeds up chemical reactions. Light energy
enables many reactions to take place, e.g.
photosynthesis and photography.

Catalysts

Hydrogen peroxide decomposition

Hydrogen peroxide H_2O_2 decomposes to form oxygen and water. The rate at which the reaction takes place can be found by collecting the oxygen formed and measuring its volume at certain times after the start of the reaction. The decomposition takes place very slowly without a catalyst, e.g. manganese(IV) oxide.

Collecting and measuring a gas

Hydrogen peroxide solution

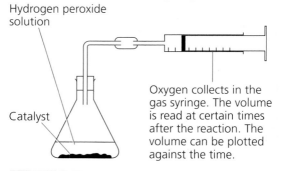

Catalyst

Oxygen collects in the gas syringe. The volume is read at certain times after the reaction. The volume can be plotted against the time.

• A catalyst is a substance which increases the rate of a chemical reaction without being used up in the reaction.
• A catalyst will catalyse a certain reaction or group of reactions. Platinum catalyses certain oxidation reactions and nickel catalyses some hydrogenation reactions.
• Catalysts are very important in industry – they enable a manufacturer to make a product more rapidly, at a lower temperature or at a lower pressure.

Enzymes

Chemical reactions take place in the cells of living things. These reactions take place reasonably fast at the temperatures which exist in plants and animals. They can do this because the cells contain powerful **catalysts** called **enzymes**. Enzymes are **proteins**; they have large molecules which are twisted into complicated three-dimensional structures. The structures are damaged by temperatures above about 45°C.

Examples of enzyme-catalysed reactions are:

Enzymes in **yeast** catalyse the conversion of sugar into ethanol and carbon dioxide. The process is called **fermentation**. It is used to make ethanol (alcohol) by the fermentation of carbohydrates. It is used to produce bubbles of carbon dioxide which make bread rise.

Enzymes in **bacteria** produce **yoghurt** from milk; they catalyse the conversion of lactose, the sugar in milk, into lactic acid.

Reaction Rates

Questions

1 Which act faster to cure acid indigestion, indigestion tablets or indigestion powders? Explain your answer.

2 Suggest three ways in which you could speed up the reaction between zinc and dilute sulphuric acid to give zinc sulphate and hydrogen. Explain why each of these methods increases the speed of the reaction.

3 (a) Someone tells you that there is an enzyme in potatoes that is better than manganese(IV) oxide as a catalyst for the decomposition of hydrogen peroxide. Describe the experiments you would do to find out whether this is true.

   (b) Why are catalysts important in industry?

4 You are asked to study the effect of temperature on this reaction.
magnesium + sulphuric acid →
          magnesium sulphate + hydrogen.
Describe the measurements you would make and what you would do with your results.

Answers

1 Powders (surface area/mass is greater). 2 Warm or use more concentrated acid or use powdered zinc. 3 (a) Compare in separate experiments, using the apparatus on page 82. (b) Allow reactions to take place at a lower temperature, saving on fuel costs or at a lower pressure, saving on the cost of the plant. 4 Measure the volume of hydrogen produced at different temperatures and plot the results to assess reaction rates.

See also   • **Rapid Revision Biology, Topic 2,** p. 35

Fossil fuels
Coal

Coal was formed from dead plant material decaying slowly over millions of years under the pressure of deposits of mud and sand. Coal is a mixture of carbon and hydrocarbons and other compounds. It is burned chiefly in power stations.

Petroleum oil and natural gas

Petroleum oil and natural gas were formed by the decay of sea animals which lived millions of years ago. Under the pressure of layers of mud and silt the organic part of the creatures turned into a mixture of hydrocarbons: petroleum oil. Pressure turned the sediment on top of the decaying matter into rock so oil is held in porous rock. Natural gas (chiefly methane) is always found in the same deposits as oil.

Industrialised countries depend on fossil fuels for transport, for power stations and for manufacturing industries. Oil is the starting material used by the petrochemicals industry to make fertilisers, herbicides, insecticides and pharmaceuticals. When we have used the Earth's deposits of coal, oil and gas there will be no more forthcoming.

See also
• p. 47 **Oxygen**
• **Rapid Revision Physics, Topic 2,** p. 26

Obtaining fuels from petroleum

Petroleum fractions and their uses

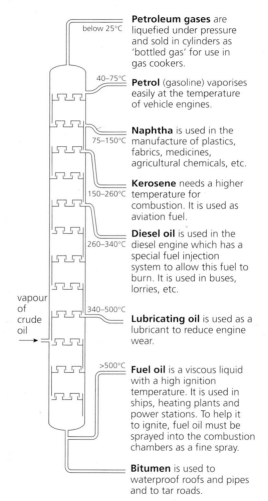

Petroleum gases are liquefied under pressure and sold in cylinders as 'bottled gas' for use in gas cookers.

below 25°C

Petrol (gasoline) vaporises easily at the temperature of vehicle engines.

40–75°C

Naphtha is used in the manufacture of plastics, fabrics, medicines, agricultural chemicals, etc.

75–150°C

Kerosene needs a higher temperature for combustion. It is used as aviation fuel.

150–260°C

Diesel oil is used in the diesel engine which has a special fuel injection system to allow this fuel to burn. It is used in buses, lorries, etc.

260–340°C

vapour of crude oil →

Lubricating oil is used as a lubricant to reduce engine wear.

340–500°C

Fuel oil is a viscous liquid with a high ignition temperature. It is used in ships, heating plants and power stations. To help it to ignite, fuel oil must be sprayed into the combustion chambers as a fine spray.

>500°C

Bitumen is used to waterproof roofs and pipes and to tar roads.

See also   • p. 19 **Apparatus for fractional distillation.**

Fuels

Cracking and alkanes

Cracking

The fractional distillation of petroleum gives many fractions. **Cracking** is used to convert the high boiling point range fractions into the lower boiling point range fractions, petrol and kerosene.

Vapour of hydrocarbon with large molecules and high b.p.

passed over a heated catalyst

(e.g. Al_2O_3 or SiO_2)

Mixture of hydrocarbons with smaller molecules and low b.p.

Alkanes

Most of the hydrocarbons in crude oil belong to the **homologous series** called **alkanes**. The compounds in a homologous series have similar chemical properties in which one member of the series differs from the next by a $-CH_2-$group. Physical properties, e.g. boiling point, vary gradually as the size of the molecules increases. Alkanes contain only single bonds between carbon atoms; they are **saturated hydrocarbons**. Members of the alkanes include methane CH_4 and ethane C_2H_6 and have the general formula C_nH_{2n+2}. Alkanes do not take part in many chemical reactions. Their important reaction is combustion; see page 88.

See also   • p. 88 **Combustion**

Energy and chemical reactions

Exothermic reactions

In exothermic reactions heat is given out (fuel, combustion, burning, see page 47).

Combustion e.g. of hydrocarbons such as methane and petroleum fractions;

methane (natural gas) + oxygen (in air) →
carbon dioxide + water

$$CH_4(g) + 2O_2(g) \rightarrow CO_2(g) + H_2O(l)$$

If there is insufficient air, combustion is incomplete and gives carbon monoxide and carbon also.

Respiration Our bodies obtain energy from the oxidation of foods, e.g. glucose in our cells. This process is called **cellular respiration**.

glucose + oxygen → carbon dioxide + water
energy is given out.

Neutralisation

hydrogen ion + hydroxide ion → water
energy is given out.

Endothermic reactions

In endothermic reactions heat is taken in.

Photosynthesis Plants take in the energy of sunlight to build sugars.

Thermal decomposition Heat is needed for e.g. cracking of hydrocarbons (see page 87) and decomposition of calcium carbonate in lime kilns to calcium oxide and carbon dioxide.

Energy diagrams

exothermic reaction: heat is given out

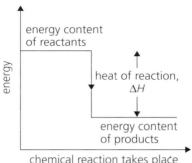

The products of the reaction contain less energy than the reactants. The reactants get rid of their extra energy by giving out heat to the surroundings.

endothermic reaction: heat is taken in

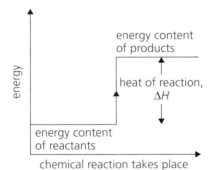

When the reactants change into the products they have to climb to a higher energy level. They take energy from (cool) the surroundings.

Energy diagrams continued

The reason why the reactants and products possess different amounts of energy is that they have different chemical bonds. Energy must be supplied to break chemical bonds in the reactants. When bonds are created in the products, energy is given out.

Exothermic reaction Energy needed to break the old bonds < energy given out when new bonds are formed.

Endothermic reaction Energy needed to break the old bonds > energy given out when new bonds are formed.

Questions

1 Draw an energy diagram for the combustion of petrol to form carbon dioxide and water. Mark the heat of reaction ΔH on your diagram, and state whether the reaction is exothermic or endothermic.

2 Draw the energy diagram for the cracking of heavy fuel oil to form kerosene. Mark the heat of reaction ΔH on your diagram and state whether the reaction is exothermic or endothermic.

Answers

1 Similar to the diagram for an exothermic reaction on page 89. 2 Similar to the diagram for an endothermic reaction on page 89.

Alkenes and their reactions

The alkenes are homologous series of hydrocarbons, including ethene C_2H_4 and propene C_3H_6 and having the general formula C_nH_{2n}. The double bond between the carbon atoms is the functional group of alkenes. Alkenes are described as **unsaturated hydrocarbons**.

Reactions of alkenes

Addition of halogens; e.g.

ethene + bromine $\rightarrow$ 1,2-dibromoethane
$$H_2C=CH_2 + Br_2 \rightarrow CH_2BrCH_2Br$$

The decolourisation of a bromine solution (brown) is used to distinguish between an alkene and an alkane. Chlorine adds to alkenes in a similar way.

Addition of water: hydration
ethene + water $\rightarrow$ ethanol
$$H_2C=CH_2 + H_2O \rightarrow C_2H_5OH$$

Ethene and steam passed over a heated catalyst under pressure give ethanol, an important industrial solvent.

Alkenes and their reactions
continued

Addition of hydrogen: hydrogenation.
Animal fats, such as butter, are saturated
compounds. Vegetable oils, such as sunflower
seed oil are unsaturated compounds. A liquid
vegetable oil can be converted into a solid fat
by hydrogenation.

		Pass over	
Vegetable	hydrogen	$\longrightarrow$	Solid
oil	+	heated	fat
(unsaturated)		nickel	(saturated)
		catalyst	

The solid fat produced is sold as margarine.

Addition polymerisation
Many molecules of the **monomer**, e.g.
ethene, **polymerise** (join together) to form
the **polymer**, e.g. poly(ethene). The
conditions needed are high pressure and a
heated catalyst.

$$nCH_2=CH_2 \xrightarrow{\text{heat, pressure, catalyst}} (-CH_2-CH_2-)_n$$

In poly(ethene), n is 30 000–40 000.
Poly(ethene) is used for making plastic bags,
for kitchenware (buckets, bowls, etc.), for
laboratory tubing and for toys. It is flexible
and difficult to break. Polymers of alkenes are
called poly(alkenes). They are **plastics**. Plastics
are strong, low-density, good insulators of
heat and electricity, resistant to attack by
chemicals, smooth and able to be moulded
into different shapes.

Thermosoftening and thermosetting plastics

There are two kinds of plastics.

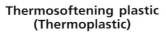

Thermosoftening plastic (Thermoplastic)

Heat: softens

hard, solid plastic   soft, pliable plastic

Cool: hardens

Thermosetting plastic

Cool: hardens

during manufacture, warm, pliable plastic   permanently hard plastic

The reason for the difference in behaviour is a difference in structure. Thermoplastics consist of long polymer chains. The forces of attraction between chains are weak.

When a thermosetting plastic sets, the chains react with one another. Cross-links are formed and a huge three-dimensional structure is built up. This is why thermosetting plastics can be formed only once.

Thermosoftening and
thermosetting plastics continued

Applications

Both types of plastic have their advantages. The material used for electrical fittings and counter tops must be able to withstand high temperatures without softening. For these purposes, **'thermosets'** are used. Sometimes gases are mixed with softened plastics to make low density plastic foam for use in car seats, thermal insulation, sound insulation and packaging. Plastics can be strengthened by the addition of other materials, e.g. the composite **glass fibre-reinforced** plastic is used for the manufacture of boat hulls and car bodies.

Poly(ethene) $(CH_2\text{-}CH_2)_n$, trade name polythene, is used to make plastic bags. High density polythene is used to make kitchenware, plastic tubing and toys.

Poly(chloroethene) $(CHCl\text{-}CH_2)_n$, trade name PVC, is used to make plastic bottles, wellingtons, raincoats, floor tiles, insulation for electrical wiring, gutters and drainpipes.

Poly(propene) is resistant to attack by chemicals and does not soften in boiling water. It can be used to make hospital equipment which needs sterilisation.

Some drawbacks of plastics

Many plastics are **non-biodegradable**. They have to be burned or dumped in landfill sites. Chemists have now developed new plastics which are biodegradable.

Plastics burn faster than wood and brick. In buildings which are insulated with plastic foam or furnished with plastic materials, fires can spread very rapidly.

Builders are not allowed to use plastics which burn to form toxic products.

Disposal of plastics waste

Recycling When plastics are recycled, there is a saving on raw materials and at the same time the pressure on disposal sites is reduced. There are problems in recycling: different types of plastic must first be separated and it is difficult to remove additives.

Fuel Plastics waste may be used as fuel.

Pyrolysis When plastics are heated in the absence of air, they are split up into products which can be separated by fractional distillation and then used in the manufacture of other materials.

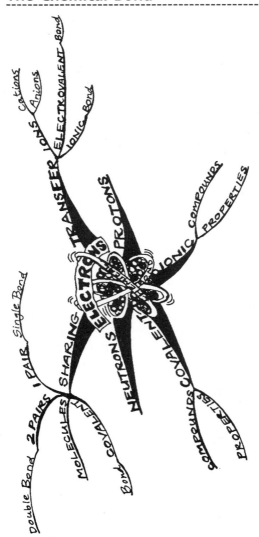